Basic Domestic Pet Library

Kittens Today
A Complete and Up-to-Date Guide

Approved by the ASPCA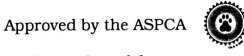

Greg Ovechka

Published in association with T.F.H. Publications, Inc.,
the world's largest and most respected publisher of pet literature

Chelsea House Publishers
Philadelphia

<u>Basic Domestic Pet Library</u>
A Cat in the Family
Amphibians Today
Aquarium Beautiful
Choosing the Perfect Cat
Dog Obedience Training
Dogs: Selecting the Best Dog for You
Ferrets Today
Guppies Today
Hamsters Today
Housebreaking and Training Puppies
Iguanas in Your Home
Kingsnakes & Milk Snakes
Kittens Today
Lovebirds Today
Parakeets Today
Pot-bellied Pigs
Rabbits Today
Turtles Today

This edition © T.F.H. Publications, Inc., 1 TFH Plaza, Neptune City, NJ 07753. This special library bound edition is made expressly for Chelsea House Publishers, a division of Main Line Book Company.

1 3 5 7 9 8 6 4 2

Library of Congress Cataloging-in-Publication Data

Ovechka, Greg.
    Kittens Today: a complete and up-to-date guide / Greg Ovechka.
       p. cm. -- (Basic domestic pet library)
    "Approved by the ASPCA"
    Includes index.
    ISBN 0-7910-4613-3 (hardcover)
1. Kittens.
I. American Society for the Prevention of Cruelty to Animals.
II. Title. III. Series.
SF447.O94 1997
636.8'07--dc21

97-3627
CIP

KITTENS TODAY

— A YEARBOOK

BY **GREG OVECHKA**
Photography: *Dr. Herbert R. Axelrod, Isabelle Francais, and Robert Pearcy*

yearBOOKS, INC.
Glen S. Axelrod
Chief Executive Officer

Mark Johnson
Vice President Sales & Marketing
Barry Duke
Chief Operating Officer

Neil Pronek
Katherine J. Carlon
Managing Editors

DIGITAL PRE-PRESS
Ken Pecca
Supervisor

John Palmer
Jose Reyes
Digital Pre-Press Production

Computer Art
Patti Escabi
Candida Moreira
Michele Newcomer

Advertising Sales
Nancy S. Rivadeneira
Advertising Sales Director
Chris O'Brien
Advertising Account Manager
Jennifer Johnson
Advertising Coordinator
Adrienne Rescinio
Advertising Production Coordinator
c yearBOOKS, Inc.
1 TFH Plaza
Neptune City, NJ 07753
Completely Manufactured in
Neptune City, NJ USA

No matter what kind of "in" pet happens to catch the pet-owning public's fancy, the cat remains among the most popular and most loved of domestic pets. People everywhere have

opened their homes and their hearts to these feline charmers, especially to young members of the species: those irresistible pouncing bundles of fluff known as kittens. However, to enjoy a kitten and see it thrive as a pet entails far more than purchasing the breed of your choice, buying it the necessary "cat things," and bringing it home.

Only with owner commitment and proper care will a kitten develop into a happy, healthy cat...and that's what this publication is all about.

WHAT ARE YearBOOKS?

Because keeping Kittens as pets is growing at a rapid pace, information on their selection, care and breeding is vitally needed in the marketplace. Books, the usual way information of this sort is transmitted, can be too slow. Sometimes by the time a book is written and published, the material contained therein is a year or two old...and no new material has been added during that time. Only a book in a magazine form can bring breaking stories and current information. A magazine is streamlined in production, so we have adopted certain magazine publishing techniques in the creation of this yearBOOK. Magazines also can be much cheaper than books because they are supported by advertising. To combine these assets into a great publication, we have issued this yearBOOK in both magazine and book format at different prices.

Silver tabby American Short-hair kittens waiting to go to their new home.

CONTENTS

KITTENS TODAY

THE APPEAL OF CATS

Cats of all ages, shapes, and sizes have made their way into the homes and hearts of millions upon millions of people. Cat lovers all have their own "pet" reasons for bringing a feline—or felines—into their homes. Some people admire the cat's intelligence; some respect the cat's spirit of independence. Still others are attracted by its grace and beauty. And almost all cat owners know what kind of good friend and companion their pet can be.

People who know cats also understand that these independent creatures will never submit entirely to their wishes, as does a dog, for example. Cat lovers understand that a pet doesn't have to be strictly obedient in order to be a good friend and companion. There's usually a sense of space in the typical—and successful—human/cat relationship: a cat takes up just a little bit of space in your home, and all he asks is that you respect it. In turn, he will allow you to go about your business with the same dignity. In the eyes of many people, cats seem to mirror human behavior, perhaps at its best.

Cats are also fascinating and interesting to watch. Few pets are as graceful. Cats are strong and powerful, yet supple and quick. It's like having a mini-jungle animal in your own living room: watching it leap from windowsills to tables, and occasionally to your shoulder, is similar to watching the "big cats" leap through trees in the jungle.

These animals are very clean; in fact, they are downright fastidious when it comes to grooming and cleaning themselves. They literally spend hours each day cleaning and washing themselves after meals; and, if you're fortunate enough to have more than one cat, grooming one another.

> **"Cat lovers understand that a pet doesn't have to be strictly obedient in order to be a good friend and companion."**

Are they intelligent? Their refusal—perhaps total lack of interest is a better way to put it—to learn tricks and come running on command or do this or that on command should not be interpreted as a lack of intelligence on their part. They are simply being logical. If they have no interest in doing your bidding, well then, why should they? Aren't they a little bit like people in that respect?

What about their gracefulness? People who appreciate beauty and gracefulness can see these attributes in the tiniest kitten and in the full-grown cat. Have you ever seen a clumsy cat? You're not likely to. The graceful cat is indeed a thing of beauty and a joy to behold. And chances are that your full-grown cat got that way by learning to play as a kitten.

One of the best things about getting a kitten, as opposed to a full-grown cat, is the opportunity it affords you to watch its development. Kittens *are* a little clumsy—they're always scurrying around, climbing up and down, and falling off your chairs or sofa, or wherever else their impish, adventurous nature takes them. Kittens are always busy: busy getting in and out of all kinds of places, busy scooting around your house, doing acrobatic flips, springing up into the air as if they were on pogo sticks—and sometimes falling flat on their faces. All this playing is good; it's a very important part of the kitten's growth and development. Play sharpens the kitten's motor skills, keeps him physically fit and in sync with the world he suddenly finds himself in. You could describe it as the feline's training program; all that activity and all that play help to develop your kitten into that powerful and graceful cat who never seems to make a mistake in his movements.

And today there is a new school of thought regarding the role that you, as kitten-owner or kitten-guardian,

"Play should, in fact, be a regular part of your relationship with your feline friend."

Cats are intelligent, inquisitive animals, and nothing escapes their attention.

should also play. Play should, in fact, be a regular part of your relationship with your feline friend. There was a time when many people believed that a kitten was simply too fragile, too delicate to play with the way you would play with a dog. In the past, many people believed that they should bring a kitten into the house and just leave it alone as if it were a fragile ornament. Many felt that you shouldn't "bother" the kitten. Nothing could be further from the truth. You *should* interact and play with your kitten. If you're afraid that the little fellow can't handle it, remember, if he's been raised the right way, he's already had his fair share of tussling and tumbling in the litter with his brothers and

sisters. Playing like this in the litter at such a tender age has already started him off on his own lifelong exercise and play program. You should help him to continue with it. Of course, you don't want to go overboard and play too rough (after all, you are much bigger than a cat, to say nothing of a tiny kitten!); and you don't want to confuse and frighten the little guy with erratic and heavy-handed movements of your own. And you should never permit very young children, under the age of four or five (depending on their level of maturity), to play with the kitten without your supervision. But you should find time to make play an integral part of his life, and of his relationship with you as a pet owner.

Speaking of that, sometimes we wish that there were a better term or expression than "pet owner" to describe the relationship between you and your cat, because the relationship is really so much more than that of "ownership." If you could think of yourself not so much as a pet "owner" but as a pet's guardian or friend or companion, it would enrich both of your lives. "Friendship from a cat?" ask some skeptics. One popular and unfortunate misconception perpetuated by certain individuals who are not "cat people" is that cats are not friendly, much less affectionate. They're great

Friends...Cats can make wonderful pets for people of all ages.

companions too. Just ask anyone who has been sidelined with an injury or an illness or is recuperating from one. They will tell you how their cats kept them company during these times. Siamese cats, for example, will probably want to spend all their time with you—they love human company and attention so much.

Being able to watch the kitten develop and grow throughout its life (and your life as well) is perhaps the number one advantage of bringing a kitten, as opposed to a mature, adult cat, into your home. There is, of course, nothing wrong with bringing home an older cat—a feline from ten months to ten years plus!—but the older the cat, the greater the chance that he's already established his own cat personality. An older cat may find adjusting to your home a little more difficult because he has already grown so accustomed to his previous environment. A kitten, on the other hand,

"Your kitten will become an integral part of your family."

A mixed-breed kitten, such as this little fellow, can make as good a pet as can a purebred.

will find adjusting to a new home and new people much easier.

And by bringing home that young kitten, you will also be able to play a greater role in helping to shape its personality. Your kitten will become an integral part of your family. Poets have, in fact, written countless odes to describe the unique human/feline relationship. For example, the Japanese haiku poet Issa wrote:

As one of us,
The cat is seated here;
The parting year.
Another intriguing thing

about kittens: while they're very much a part of your family, they're still, at the same time, related to the fascinating cat family. When you see a black panther, snow leopard, or lion, glance over at the tiny black kitten, white domestic shorthair, or fluffy Persian with his mane. They're all mini-versions of these awesome creatures—and they live right in your very own home!

Intelligence, playfulness, beauty, companionship, friendship, power, and strength—these and many other attributes characterize most felines from the time they are the tiniest kittens. If you appreciate and treasure all of these marvelous qualities in a pet, then a cat is just right for you.

KITTENS TODAY

SELECTING A KITTEN

Everyone loves a kitten—It's a cute, adorable, tiny, cuddly ball of fur. But this "precious" little kitten will become a full-grown cat by the time it's nine months old. That's something that some people forget to consider when they bring a kitten home. They discover that they adored the kitten, but lose interest in it when it reaches the cat stage. Please don't do this—for your sake and for your kitten's sake. Get a kitten only if you can make a lifelong commitment to it. Your kitten will grow from infancy to the equivalent of childhood and then to young adulthood in just 12 months. And if you give it the proper care, it will spend many happy years with you.

Your commitment to your kitten will involve many things, in addition to providing the basics, which are good food, a clean litter box, proper health care, and grooming. For instance, while I attempt to write this piece, my Siamese insists on sitting on the pages and is not very happy with my moving him. Would this sort of thing bother you? If it would, you may not be

Eight-week-old Siamese kittens. The Siamese is one of the most popular cat breeds.

prepared for the type of commitment we're talking about here.

You should also make sure that every member of your family is going to be willing to make this commitment to the feline member of the family. How many times have we heard the story of the parent who goes out and brings home a kitten for his child, only to discover that the child doesn't like kittens, or that neither parent nor child is

> **"Get a kitten only if you can make a lifelong commitment to it."**

interested in taking the time needed to provide the proper care and supervision that the kitten needs. Kittens are not toys; they're more like little babies. They need to be fed three, four, even five times a day. They need a lot of supervision. You, or someone in your family, must be there for the little guy. If your family is not prepared to give that kitten just a bit of time and energy, you would perhaps be better off leaving all of the responsibilities—and joys—of kitten ownership to others who will be very willing to do so.

As far as I'm concerned, another unforgivable sin is the decision by a family that is expecting a baby to get rid of the cat when the new member of the family arrives, or even before. Many mothers and fathers are under the false impression that they must get rid of their feline pet at this time because the animal will jeopardize the health of the mother and threaten the well-being of the infant. This is sheer nonsense. If you are planning to have a family, or are planning to expand your family, simply include in your planning program a procedure wherein you will keep the kitten out of the nursery. No, the kitten will not "take your infant's breath away," as the old false notion goes. Of course, if you have a kitten and a baby in the same home, you should not leave the kitten alone in the room where the baby is sleeping. This is not to say that the kitten is planning harm. In fact, kittens generally love babies and children, but your pet might, in fact, try to cuddle up to the baby in its crib. This may sound adorable, but it is not advisable. Wait until both are a little older; they'll have plenty of time to become good friends. If you have a newborn, or are planning to, *don't* get rid of your cat.

What's the right age for children to be left alone with a kitten? This really varies according to the relative maturity level of the child,

This unique-looking breed, known as the Sphynx, is characterized by its hairless coat.

something which very often has less to do with the age of the child than it does with the child's personality. Some children become much more responsible and mature at an earlier age than others. Some children know how to treat animals. Others may play too rough. Some can be too enthusiastic, thoughtless, or careless about the way they handle small animals. Rule no. 1 for pet owners or pet guardians is *Know Your Animal.* Rule no. 2 along those lines might be *Know Your Child.*

There are several other points to take into consideration before you go out to purchase your kitten. Make sure that you are not allergic to cats. Some people know they like cats and are willing to accept all the responsibilities involved in taking care of them properly—but they find out

when it is too late that they are almost uncontrollably allergic to them. This does not mean that you, if you are allergic, cannot become less sensitive to cat hair. In many cases, a routine vacuuming of the carpets and a good washing and waxing of the floors will prevent allergic reactions to cat hair. But if, unfortunately, you are one of those people who will simply be unable to tolerate an allergic reaction to cat hair, you should find this out *before* you bring a kitten into your home.

How can you determine if you are allergic to felines? Perhaps by spending some

"Kittens are not toys; they're more like little babies. They need to be fed three, four, even five times a day. They need a lot of supervision."

time at a friend's or relative's house where there are a couple of cats. And make sure to give it the real test: go there during the winter when the windows are closed.

And finally, we would also ask you, the prospective guardian and friend of your kitten, to take into consideration this factor: If you are planning to move to another home, or from a house to an apartment, or from one part of the country to another, will you be willing to bring your pet along? If your answer is "Yes," or "Of course," then I think that we'd all agree that you have all of the makings of being a good friend and guardian for your kitten.

ONE KITTEN OR TWO?

How many kittens should you have in your home? Obviously, there's no rule governing the matter. But I would suggest that if you are planning to bring *one* member of the feline family into your home, you should seriously consider providing it with a brother or sister. I recommend—in fact, I highly recommend—the two-kitten household for a number of what I believe are very good reasons. First of all, let me address the arguments *against* this idea: many people argue that a new kitten is going to be *their* companion, and that all the kitten needs is a family that cares about it and provides love, comfort, security, and warmth. But there's another

factor to consider and that is: you simply will not be able to be with the kitten all the time, probably not even

Young children should always be supervised when they are in the presence of the family cat, or any other family pet for that matter.

as much as you would like to be in today's busy, fast-paced world. So, what happens to the kitten when you have to go away for that three-day weekend or that business trip? What about a situation whereby you leave early in the morning to go to work or school and don't come home until late in the evening? One kitten is probably going to get a bit lonely at these times when you are away and he is left all alone in the house. And chances are that with no one to play with, it will not remain as active as it once was in its early days—playing in the litter with its

brothers and sisters. Well, we all know how important it is to stay active. If you provide a kitten with a playmate and friend, you will really be doing him—and yourself—a big favor. If you work or go to school, they can keep each other company during the day. This means that you won't feel so guilty when you are forced to stay late at the

"...if you are planning to bring *one* member of the feline family into your home, you should seriously consider providing it with a brother or sister."

If you have two cats, they will probably bond more closely with each other than with you.

Abyssinian and Burmese kittens checking out the view from the backyard fence.

This pair of Abyssinian kittens displays all the charming qualities of their breed.

office, or go right out to a restaurant after work, or shop, or do other errands and don't get home until late in the evening.

The best thing about it is that cats are so easy to care for. You would need lots of room for two dogs, for example. But two cats are as easy to have in your home as is one.

You should, however, take age into consideration if you are planning a two-feline home. Let's say that you already have a cat. Should you bring another one into your home? By all means, but I should be quick to point out that, from my experience, their ages should not be too far apart. For example, if you have a ten-year-old cat, it might not be the best idea to bring home a kitten. And it is not a good idea to bring an older cat—one whose

personality has already been formed—into a home where a "senior" cat is already in residence.

I would suggest, after observing some of the different ways in which kittens and cats get along with one another, that they be perhaps two to five years apart in age. For instance, if you have a five-year-old cat, you might want to consider bringing home a kitten. An ideal age range, I believe, is the two-year-old cat and the new kitten of eight weeks of age. Of course, there are exceptions to this rule, e.g., stories of older cats getting along famously with kittens and so on, but this advice is offered as a rule of thumb.

Another very important point: make sure that both felines have been neutered

"If you provide a kitten with a playmate and friend, you will really be doing him—and yourself—a big favor."

or spayed. Unaltered cats, when fully grown, are likely to fight with neutered males and even with spayed females. Desexed pets, however, usually get along very well with one another...That is, if they have been introduced in the proper way.

Mixed-breed kittens. Never purchase a kitten that is under eight weeks of age.

The right way, the *only* way, to introduce the newcomer to the present feline occupant of your home is *slowly!* First of all, put the older cat in a closed room before you even open the front door and bring in your kitten. Then you should permit the new guy to gradually become familiar with your house on his own. This will also give him the chance to become familiar with the scent of your other cat. Scent is a very important factor in the adjustment process that they have to make toward one another before they will accept the presence of one another and not view it as a threat.

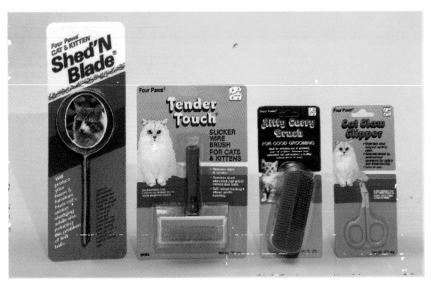

Pet shops carry a variety of grooming tools that will help to keep your cat looking its best. Photo courtesy of Four Paws.

After a while, trade places. Put the new arrival in another part of your home and allow your other cat to become familiar with the kitten's scent. Basically, you are starting to bring them together by first of all keeping them apart!

If you attempt to speed up or rush this period of adjustment, they will probably take even longer to become friends. I emphasize this point—the need for patience on your part—because we have heard about uninformed individuals who have gone out and brought a new kitten home and dropped him right in the middle of the living room where their older cat is busy grooming himself on the sofa, as if to say, "Hey Morris, here's a new friend for you!" As if the two would shake hands and hit it off right

then and there! This, of course, is the *wrong* way to go about introducing two animals. Cats are extremely territorial toward one another at first. If they could read and write, they'd probably have their name all over the house as if to say, "This is mine!" They view the newcomer as you would perhaps view an uninvited guest.

The object is to introduce them very slowly. Be patient. It may take days, possibly even weeks, and maybe even

"Cats are extremely territorial toward one another at first."

months before the two felines start to really get used to one another and decide, perhaps, to be good buddies. You should not push them on one another because throughout this time of adjustment, both of them will, naturally, be nervous, skittish, and jumpy.

Time will bring them together. You can help out a little with a few tricks of your own. Some suggest that you set up some kind of screen door separating the two cats, but allowing each

Cats and dogs can become the best of friends if they are introduced early on. This kitten and puppy already are quite comfortable with each other.

to see the other at the same time. You can do this through the use of a screen, glass, or thermoplastic door as a buffer. This method also enables you to observe the way the two felines are getting on. You probably will even be able to *hear* the way they are hitting it off by the sounds that they make. If they're still hissing at each other, there's still a long way to go.

Now you might be saying, "Gee whiz, it's so much easier to have just one kitten in the house!" So why go through all of this trouble? And why put both felines through so much of an ordeal? Sure, it's a lot of work, but think about how nice it is to have a friend, think about how you appreciate good company. And take into account the fact that cats do too. The author can recall this very vividly in snapshots of Tom, an all-white domestic shorthair, and Chipper, a frisky seal-point Siamese two years younger than Tom. In every picture— hundreds of them literally— the two are seen nuzzled up nose to nose on those cold, gray winter days—or those chilly afternoons in late fall and early spring. Every evening, they'd run around

A playful swipe is often part of getting acquainted. For the most part, such encounters end amicably.

the house chasing one another from room to room. The next thing you know, they would be tumbling, rolling and wrestling. Then they would stop and kind of relax in that position: with

Cats and rabbits can also be friends. This kitten and his Dutch rabbit pal are about to explore the garden.

Chipper nuzzled against Tom's belly. Such good buddies!

There are no guarantees that two cats will always become such good friends, but in most cases, the two-cat relationship will work. In some cases, the two will keep their distance and leave one another alone. In other cases, they will become friends, and in others they will be lifelong companions.

Again, consider the age factor, something that the author also learned when we tried to bring home an eight-week-old kitten as a friend for out ten-year-old cat. There was simply too much of an age difference between the two. The kitten wanted to play, fight, and tussle. The older one didn't, and the two simply tolerated each other. Not to let it go at that, when this kitten reached the age of two, we brought in a young stray that we literally found on the street one very cold winter's night. The newcomer established early on that she would handle all the tumbling and tussling

Maine Coon kittens.

Safe and sound in the arms of his canine companion, this cat hasn't a care in the world.

Children should be taught the right way to handle a kitten: gently but securely.

helpless creature. The grown cat is a different story. The older cat—even a one-year-old—and the older dog that is already a long-standing member of the family may see each other as rivals for the family's attention and affection. You'd probably be better off bringing home a kitten, rather than a grown cat, if you already have a dog.

And if you do bring a kitten home to live with you and your dog, be sure to follow the very same steps you would take if you were introducing two felines. Introduce them very slowly so that they can become familiar with each other's scent. A dog's bark can be an intimidating force, and

that the two-year-old wanted. Now they are companions, and our oldest cat can be left alone, which is what he prefers.

A NEW KITTEN AND OTHER ANIMALS?

If you already have a dog, you might be wondering if it's all right to bring a new kitten into your home. The first thing you'll probably have to put out of your mind is the old false notion that the two will "fight like cats and dogs." No, canine and feline are not natural enemies. They will, in fact, live together in perfect harmony, as they do in millions of homes.

The adult dog rarely gives the young kitten any problems. In fact, the dog might even become somewhat protective over what he perceives as a tiny,

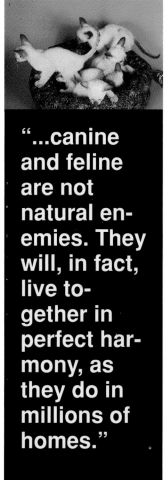

"...canine and feline are not natural enemies. They will, in fact, live together in perfect harmony, as they do in millions of homes."

dogs are usually much bigger and stronger. However, even the tiniest kitten can be a tricky fellow with his set of very sharp claws "up his sleeve." Make sure that you trim the kitten's claws in case there's an unanticipated outburst.

How long will it take before you can leave your kitten and dog alone together? There's no sure way of answering this question beforehand. It will be up to you to use your good judgment and decide when the time is right.

MALE OR FEMALE KITTEN?

Another thing to think about before you adopt a new kitten: do you want a male or female? First of all, it should be pointed out that members of both sexes

15

Cats are the best pets in the world...Just ask any cat lover!

make terrific pets—if they are treated right and given the proper care. There are, of course, physical differences between the two. Females are usually smaller, more dainty or "ladylike" in appearance than are males. They are also a little "rounder" or "softer" than are males. It's really a matter of personal preference. Acquaint yourself with a few kittens at a friend's or relative's house. See if you can notice any basic differences; decide for yourself which you would prefer. Maybe you would want one of each.

Finally, always keep in mind that whenever you do bring a new kitten, or any other animal for that matter, into your home, the animal

should be in good health. This is especially relevant if you already have other animals at home. The last thing that you want to do is bring in a sick animal. Many

"...always keep in mind that whenever you do bring a new kitten into your home, the animal should be in good health."

a disease has been transmitted through the common use of the same litter box, or the same food or water bowl. Kittens, for example, are highly susceptible to worms, which can be transmitted to other cats that use the same litter box. If there is any doubt in your mind, it might be a good idea to quarantine the new kitten. Keep litter boxes and food and water dishes separate—until you are sure that the kitten is absolutely free from infections, parasites, or skin problems. If your new kitten happens to be a stray that you found in the neighborhood, make sure that you take it to the vet for a clean bill of health before you bring it home. This cannot be overemphasized: animal diseases are highly *contagious!*

KITTENS TODAY

BREEDS

We don't hold to the view that one breed of kitten is better than another. We believe, in fact, that given the proper care, all kittens can become true "aristocats." Of course, there are differences between the breeds. Cat lovers know that one of the most difficult things about selecting a kitten is narrowing down their choice from a fascinating variety of breeds, ranging from the exotic to the domestic, from the shorthair to the longhair, from the all white to the all black, and even the all blue. There are so many different breeds with so many beautiful coats, colors, features, and different personalities that many a cat fancier has simply shrugged and said, "I wish I could take them *all* home with me!" Well, unless you happen to live on a very big ranch or farm, you will simply be unable to do this...Although many have tried! If you're like most folks, you will have to make a choice.

If you are thinking about getting a purebred, you will

Oh say can you see...the world of purebred cats?

have to set aside much more time—and money—to find the one that you want. Also, you should

"If you are thinking about getting a pure-bred, you will have to set aside much more time—and money—to find the one that you want."

understand that it takes a lot of time and money to produce these cats. That extra money goes to help cover all of the breeding costs, including purchase and care of the mother, stud fee for the father, care of the mother during pregnancy, veterinary fees, tender loving care of the kittens after birth, inoculations, documentation, and other expenses. The costs involved in breeding these purebreds are much greater than most people would think.

If you want to get some idea about the prices that purebreds command, you can, of course, stop in at your local pet shop or visit a breeder. Other ways to give you some ballpark estimates: look through a copy of a cat association magazine or other pet publications. They will usually list current prices that purebreds are selling for on the market.

Abyssinian kitten. The coat markings are not yet fully developed.

Another good way to find out more about purebreds is to attend a cat show. Hundreds of cat shows are held every year throughout the country. There you will be able to meet breeders and also see a dazzling display of different show cats. Now all you have to do is to choose from so many fascinating breeds! We will try to refrain from calling each a beauty—but they all are! The following is but a *small* sampling of the

The Abyssinian, or Aby, comes in a number of colors, each of which is distinguished by a ticked pattern.

various cat breeds from which you can choose.

ABYSSINIAN

You might have seen this exotic cat in the art and sculpture of the ancient Egyptians, who elevated it

"The Abyssinian's striking appearance resembles that of the African wild cat."

to the status of sacred animal. The Abyssinian's striking appearance resembles that of the African wild cat. He has large ears with pointed tips and looks as if he were listening for something out in the wilderness. His green eyes will gaze at you from out of the mythic past.

In addition to these special qualities, you'll be pleased to note that in your living room he will conduct himself in a quiet, gentle manner, and will communicate in a soft, melodious voice. Like the Siamese, he is recognized for his fondness for human companionship and for his intelligence. He "talks" like the Siamese—but not as much or as loud.

Like the Siamese, he has also made a name for himself on the show circuit with his warm, glowing colors and soft, silky coat. His short coat is something like that of a hare's coat and because of this

colors appearing at about the age of one. Other Burmese color varieties are blue, champagne, and platinum.

The Burmese is similar to the Siamese but stockier in appearance. It is medium sized, graceful looking, yet muscular. The rather small head, rounded at the top, tapers to a short, distinctive muzzle. The round-shaped eyes are set wide apart and are yellow or golden in color.

The Burmese is a very affectionate, playful, gentle—and also vocal—feline.

A Burmese will typically show good muscular development, even at the kitten stage. With his expressive eyes and sweet expression, the Burmese has its own unique appearance. Members of this breed are outgoing and pleasant tempered. They can make fine feline companions.

similarity, he sometimes has been called the "bunny cat." Like the Siamese, the Abyssinian kitten loses none of its famous playfulness when it becomes an adult.

When you do get to know this brown or copper-red kitten with its bands of dark and light fur, you'll be sure to admire him and consider him for your pet.

Burmese kittens. The Burmese is an intelligent cat with a charming personality.

The Burmese is actually the result of a cross between an Oriental-type cat and a Siamese. It comes in a number of colors, the best known of which is sable brown.

BURMESE

The Burmese is a close cousin of the Siamese, which it resembles except in color. The coat of the Burmese is fine and satiny in texture, chocolate brown or sable in color. Like the Siamese, the Burmese sports a lighter coat toward the upper underbody, and the coat darkens below that. The most well-known color variety of the Burmese is dark brown, with the points, including the Siamese-like face-mask, a richer seal brown. Kittens are lighter, with their true

HIMALAYAN

Its Persian and Siamese ancestry is readily apparent in the Himalayan. It has a thick, long, fluffy coat like the Persian, and the color and points of the Siamese. A regular on the cat show circuit, the Himalayan, or Himmy, is also a prize winner in the home because of its warm, affectionate personality.

Color varieties include seal point, blue point, chocolate point, lilac point, and red. If your Himalayan kitten appears somewhat on the pale side, that's perfectly normal; those colors will darken with age.

Like the Siamese, the Himalayan has brilliant blue eyes, but not so the Siamese voice—a fact that some say is to the advantage of the Himalayan!

The Himalayan is a hybrid cross between the Siamese and the Persian. Its coloration can be either solid or pointed.

KORAT

This cat is distinguished by its silvery blue coloration. The Korat is medium sized and muscular. It has dense, soft fur. Its large greenish-gold eyes are a striking feature.

"A regular on the cat show circuit, the Himalayan, or Himmy, is also a prize winner in the home because of its warm, affectionate personality."

The face of the Korat is heart shaped; the muzzle is sharp but not pointed. The ears are large; the tips are rounded. The blunt-tipped tail is of medium length.

Himalayan kitten. This impressive-looking breed sports a gorgeous flowing coat.

The silver-blue beauty known as the Korat has an ancient history that originates in Thailand (formerly Siam). Its large, round green eyes are one of its most striking features.

The Korat is mellow and mild mannered. Truly a laid-back cat.

Maine Coon kittens. The feathering on the ears is characteristic of the breed.

In addition to being a show cat, the Korat–a word that means "silver" in Thai—is popular as a pet because it is affectionate and responsive to people.

MAINE COON CAT

The Maine Coon cat can boast of a number of tales

Maine Coon. This breed, which hails from New England, is a hardy cat whose coat helps it to withstand the rugged winters of Maine.

that explain its creation, including it being the result of a housecat/raccoon mating, but in all probability its origin lies with early New England housecats and imported longhairs that were likely Angora.

The Maine Coon is a powerfully built feline with medium-length hair. It has a big head, large ears, and yellowish oval eyes. These cats sport a prominent ruff, a protective layer of "clothing," you might say, for the cold Maine winter climate.

Aside from the raccoon-coat patterns, Maine Coon coats also come in solid and mixed colors. The size difference between male and female members of the breed can be quite noticeable.

MANX

Most everyone knows the Manx by its lack of a tail and by its rabbit-like hop. The Manx's back legs are much longer and

"The Maine Coon cat can boast of a number of tales that explain its creation, including it being the result of a housecat/raccoon mating..."

21

Manx. Taillessness is the distinguishing characteristic of this unusual breed, which supposedly originated on the Isle of Man.

The Manx's rear legs are shorter than those in the front, which is why the Manx hops about in a rabbit-like fashion.

more powerful than are the front legs. Manx cats are compact and sturdy, with good musculation.

The large eyes and pronounced cheekbones add to the attractive quality of the face.

The Manx's coat is short, soft, and dense. It comes in a rainbow of striking colors including blue smoke, chinchilla, silver patched tabby, and red.

While all of these qualities draw attention to the Manx, what really sells people on this breed is its affectionate, intelligent nature.

PERSIAN

As the Siamese is one of the most popular, if not *the* most popular of the

Persian kitten. The elegant appearance of this breed has won it a steady, devoted following in the cat fancy.

"The Persian conveys the impression of elegance, whether its coat of arms is all white, all black, all blue, all red, or all cream."

Cobby and well muscled, the Persian is a cat of substance. The thick, profuse coat adds to the imposing appearance of the breed.

tabbies, shadeds, Persians that have "tipped" fur or black tips on white fur for the chinchilla and shaded silver; and red or cream tipping for the cameos. The smoke Persian has a white undercoat with fur that is heavily tipped with black, red, or blue.

And did we mention the exotic eyes of the Persian? Many Persians have eyes of two different colors, for example, one eye may be copper, and the other one blue.

They are gentle, these Persians; and if you also appreciate beauty, grace, and strength in an animal, a Persian kitten may be just right for you.

shorthair purebreds, the Persian is one of the most popular of the longhair purebreds. And what a difference in the appearance of these two popular cats! The Persian, with its soft, luxuriant coat, looks like a miniature lion with his mane across the neck and back and his small ears set wide apart on his massive, round head. His broad-chested body is set low on sturdy legs, giving an impression of strength and solidity. His ears are furry inside and out, and he has tufts of fur between his paws.

The Persian conveys the impression of elegance, whether its coat of arms is all white, all black, all blue, all red, or all cream. In addition to the striking solid colors, there are

REX

There are a number of varieties of Rex, including the Cornish, the Devon, the German, and the Oregon. It is the Cornish variety that first displayed the rex mutation, appearing in a kitten in a litter in Cornwall, England in 1950. The Rex mutation is characterized by a wavy coat that looks as if it had

Overall, the Rex has a lean look. It has a wedge-shaped head, medium- to large- sized eyes, and large pointed ears. Not all that many people have a Rex in their homes, but as word keeps spreading about the delightful qualities of this unique-looking breed, more and more homes will welcome him.

RUSSIAN BLUE

Mystery surrounds the origin of the Russian Blue, but's it's no mystery at all why generations of cat fanciers have made this blue beauty their favorite. The slate-blue color of the coat is deep, rich, and free of shading, presenting an absolutely elegant appearance that goes nicely with the bright green eyes.

just been permed at the beauty salon...Even the whiskers are curled! The Rex responds very nicely to people and makes an excellent pet. And its short, easy-to-care-for coat requires just a few gentle strokes with a coat cloth to look its best.

"The Rex responds very nicely to people and makes an excellent pet."

Above: Brown Cornish Rex. The curly coat of the Rex is the result of a mutation. *Facing page:* Devon Rex. While the Rex isn't on the top-ten list of popular cats, it does have a devoted following among those who find it to be a most delightful pet.

Russian Blue. The roots of this breed are not known for certain, but some believe that it originated in Archangelsk, Russia, from where it ultimately was imported into Great Britain.

The Russian Blue's deep green eyes contrast beautifully with the blue coat, which can vary somewhat in its shading.

The sleek and graceful Russian Blue is affectionate, intelligent, and has a mellow disposition. It is a joy to have around the house.

SIAMESE

Where should I start when describing this remarkable cat? The colors, the companionship (our Siamese is at this moment literally curled up next to my typewriter, as he has been for hours), the remarkable personality...

The distinctive appearance of the Siamese has won the hearts of many in the cat fancy. Its narrow, wedge-shaped head tapers down from its ears to its somewhat pointed muzzle, and its almond-shaped brilliant deep blue eyes are slanted down toward the nose. The body is medium sized and compact. In general conformation it is lean and lithe.

Attractive indeed are the Siamese color varieties. At birth, Siamese kittens are almost all white, with the "points" (the color on the face-mask, ears, paws, and tail) appearing later. The points contrast nicely with the lighter color of the body coat color. There's the seal point Siamese with his rich, cream-colored coat and points of seal or black-brown. There's also the chocolate point, with a paler, lighter cream-colored coat and points the color of milk chocolate. The blue

An inquisitive litter of Siamese kittens. The Siamese, which is one of the most popular breeds of cat, is said to be the closest thing to a dog—in a cat.

point Siamese is bluish white, with darker blue points. And last, there is the lilac point, which is unshaded white with frosty pinkish-gray points.

As all Siamese kittens get older, their coats also darken a bit. Whatever color its coat is, the

"The personality of the Siamese sets it apart from many other breeds."

Siamese will keep it immaculately clean!

The personality of the Siamese sets it apart from many other breeds. "He's just like a dog!" exclaimed one visitor who saw our Siamese come running when he was being called.

Long, lithe, and lean aptly describe the conformation of the Siamese. Shown here is a seal point, which is one of the four colors for the Siamese. (The other colors are chocolate point, lilac point, and blue point.)

Attending cat shows is an excellent way to learn about cat breeds and to determine which breed is the right one for you. Here, a Himalayan is being judged.

"Siamese are very vocal and sound very much like a baby."

"Think that's something? Well, watch this," we told our guest, as we tossed a grapevine across the room. Our Siamese set off for it at once, picked it up with his teeth, returned to where we were standing, and dropped it at our feet.

A Siamese is very active. Ours will fetch, come running when you call it, and even—when he hears the sound of a package from the deli being opened—sit up and beg for a choice morsel!

The Siamese that we have known have also relished a nice piece of freshly cooked turkey or chicken, not to mention a succulent piece of steamed flounder. Don't be at all surprised if your Siamese regularly comes running to the kitchen when dinner is being served!

Another unique aspect of this breed is that it "talks!" Siamese are very vocal and sound very much like a baby. We can't begin to count the times when people on the other end of the phone have asked, "Is that a baby crying somewhere?" And we've had to tell them, "That's no baby—that's our Siamese." You would be surprised at how many people won't believe it!"

Yes, the Siamese cries for attention, for food—even for you to stop whatever you're doing and put the TV on and sit down—so that it can curl up in your lap. Siamese are *very* demanding at times; and, perhaps for this reason, they've gotten a reputation in some quarters as being mean. They're not mean; they're just very sociable, alert, and sensitive. And sometimes when they don't get their way, they can act like babies—crying or whining. It would be no exaggeration to say that the analogy is apt: many people who have Siamese kittens really do treat them as if they were human babies.

If that sounds a bit much, consider the way the King of Siam (now Thailand) treated them. According to legend, the King of Siam considered his Siamese cats to be sacred guardians of the temple and suitable companions for the priests. Word got out about these remarkable creatures, and they were soon shipped to England. Around 1890, they were first brought to the US; and from the time of their show debut just after the turn of the century, they began to capture the imagination of the American people. Today they are among the most popular of all cats. When you see that tiny Siamese kitten, think of all that!

PEDIGREES

If you are planning to bring home a purebred kitten, be sure that you receive a copy of the kitten's pedigree, which is a written listing of its ancestors. Keep it safely filed away, because

Siamese are alert, active cats that are keenly interested in the world around them.

"If you are planning to bring home a purebred kitten, be sure that you receive a copy of the kitten's pedigree, which is a written listing of its ancestors."

someday you may need it.

Initially, a person might think that he is interested in a kitten only as a housepet. But in many cases, that kitten will start to get so many compliments from visitors that his owner starts to consider exhibiting his pride and joy on the show circuit. If this is the case, the kitten's pedigree and registration papers will have to be presented before he is accepted for showing.

Another thing: If you are buying a purebred kitten, make sure that the breeder or pet shop manager agrees that your kitten can be returned within a certain amount of time, perhaps 48 or 72 hours, if it does not pass a veterinarian's examination for health and

29

soundness. No reputable breeder or pet shop owner will sell you a kitten that is in poor health—after all, they have a reputation to maintain. Last, but not least, never allow anyone to pressure you into a sale. Head for the door if you feel that this is happening.

THE NON-PUREBRED KITTEN

First of all, I would like to repeat: all cats, even non-purebreds, are aristocats. Our cat Boo, an all-black domestic shorthair, is a wonderful example of such a cat.

He was found half frozen on the side of the road on a cold winter night by a Good Samaritan who just happened to be driving by and who spotted the tiny, helpless creature. This same person put the kitten into his car and drove it to a veterinarian for first-aid. When the kitten started to regain some of its strength, the vet brought him over to the local SPCA. He had lost a lot of hair from frostbite, and his skin was irritated and very raw. But our friends—and Boo's—at the animal shelter wined him and dined him with their most nutritious kitten food and milk. They even put a hot water bottle in his cage to keep him warm. One day, we wandered over to the SPCA and saw him for the first time. As soon as his cage was opened, he made a flying leap for our shoulders and started

Play posture. If this cat (a non-purebred) was being aggressive, its claws would be extended.

purring affectionately. We knew right then and there that this little kitten was for us. The shelter still wanted to give him some more time to recuperate, and when they finally agreed that he was well enough and on the road to recovery, they allowed him to leave and turned him over to us. Today, thanks to all of the special care and attention he received in his hours of need, he is a healthy cat with a thick, glossy coat;

most of all, he is a wonderful pet. And perhaps because of all of the help that he got from people, he is extremely friendly.

Finally, what if a friend or a neighbor "finds" a kitten (a stray) for you? This kitten can also become a good pet. The one difference here is that its history is totally unknown to you. It may be basically healthy, but it might need shots or de-worming. Before bringing in a stray, you really should take him straight to the vet. It is especially important that the kitten be given a clean bill of health if you already have cats or other animals in your home.

In their own way, non-pure-bred kittens can be just as attractive as can purebreds.

A bright-eyed mixed breed kitten. Even though your prospective new kitty appears to be the picture of good health, it still should have a veterinary check-up.

KITTENS TODAY

IS YOUR KITTEN HEALTHY?

Your most important priority when obtaining a kitten is to select one that is healthy. Be sure to look for the following signs of good health when making your choice: clear eyes, free of irritation, tearing or other discharge; clean ears, free of mites and other foreign matter; firm, pink gums, free of sores; and a nice full coat with no bare spots.

A kitten with a runny nose or eyes could sometimes be prone to illness in the long run. And a kitten that sneezes a lot might also mean frequent trips to the vet later on. If you like a certain kitten, but have your doubts about its health, ask the breeder or pet shop manager if it would be all right to bring the animal over to your vet's for a brief general examination.

Of course everyone wants that champ of a kitten that is running around and jumping up and down, "bright-eyed and bushy-tailed," as the saying goes. Try calling a kitten that you're interested in and see if it responds. In addition, you might try clapping your hands or making noises to see if a kitten looking in the other direction responds. This can be a good way to test the kitten's hearing.

If a kitten is unusually skittish or spits and hisses occasionally, don't take it personally. It simply may be frightened of you and/or its new surroundings. However, if the kitten seems frightened and hisses continuously, or if he seems to scratch or bite aggressively, there may be other personality problems; and you could have a problem attempting to gain its trust. It would not be wise to bring this animal into a household with small children.

A kitten may meow for a number of reasons. This little fellow hasn't eaten for several hours, and he's hungry.

Generally speaking, the physically sound kitten is active and alert. Even at an early age, it will try to make its way around to see what's going on around it. All cats are naturally curious and intelligent; but, as with people, some cats are more curious and intelligent than are others.

When selecting your new kitten, you should also consider, in addition to the general health of the kitten itself, the cleanliness of the premises in which he was raised. You might also want to ask about the health of your kitten's parents, as well as that of its brothers and sisters.

Whatever route you follow to find that special kitten that you have in

"Generally speaking, the physically sound kitten is active and alert."

mind, you will always remember that trip back to your home—with your new kitten—as a particularly memorable day in your life.

Above: American Shorthair kittens. Playing is more than just having fun; it is an important part of a kitten's growth and development. *Below:* Female Japanese Bobtail, black and white bicolor.

When choosing a kitten, check for the following: bright clear eyes with no signs of discharge, a dry nose, and clean ears, with no signs of foreign matter.

Birman kitten taking some time to sniff the posies. Remember that your kitty will need time to become acclimated to its new environment.

KITTENS TODAY

BRINGING YOUR KITTEN HOME

Yes, that first day your kitten arrives in your home is truly an exciting one in so many ways for both you and your pet. And at this exciting time, you should not forget to have everything ready for the newcomer. You should have a warm, cozy, quiet, out-of-the-way place for the kitten to sleep. In fact, it might be a very good idea to bring the kitten to a safe, quiet place in your home and make him feel instantly relaxed and secure.

This quiet, peaceful, soothing setting should also be away from drafts and up off the floor a few inches at least. Floors can be very drafty. Even though you yourself cannot feel the draft, chances are that it is there just the same. Drafts are sneaky: under most conditions animals and people can adjust to cold and heat, but they can't tolerate drafts. If you line your kitten's bed with a soft, comfortable pillow, you'll keep him away from those nasty drafts. Remember, the cozier the

A cat's power of concentration can be very intense. With claws extended, this cat waits for the opportune moment to make his move.

"**You should have a warm, cozy, quiet, out-of-the-way place for the kitten to sleep.**"

bed the better. After all, up to this time that kitten has had his mother and his littermates to snuggle up to.

Speaking of litter, the term is used in two ways in the world of cats and kittens: as another word for the kitten's earliest family; or as in litter pan, to which he should also be introduced as soon as you bring him to his new quarters in your home.

What else should you have ready for the new kitten that first day? Clean fresh water in a sturdy, non-tippable dish and a supply of kitten chow.

37

strange and tired. Let him take a nap if he likes. Just keep an eye on him—as you would an important guest.

Probably the most important thing you should tell all members of your family is that the new kitten is really a lot like a baby. Everyone should be careful when they are near the little guy that first day or two. Little children should be told that loud, rambunctious play and loud noises can easily scare a new kitten and possibly make him into a nervous little fellow. You and your family *should* play and interact with your kitten, but "easy does it" is the best thing for starters. Give the young pet a little time to gradually get used to all family members before expecting it to maintain the daily routine of work and play. In no time at all, he'll have the run of the house and will feel right at home.

Never, never introduce the kitten to your home by slapping or hitting him if he has an accident—by the litter pan, for example. Never hit a kitten as a disciplinary measure. If you are inclined toward using some form of punishment as a way of training, the most extreme step you should take is to say "No" in a voice he will learn to understand. In general, kittens simply do not respond to threats and to punishment. It doesn't work on them. Kindness and logic are the best approaches you should take to "bringing up kitty." For

Rope and similar items are not suitable as cat toys. They could get snagged on something, and the cat might not be able to free itself.

"Never, never introduce the kitten to your home by slapping or hitting him if he has an accident by the litter for example."

But for starters, do not expect too much of the new kitten. He may be a little bewildered, less inclined to play, and more interested in making sure his new quarters are safe and secure. He may even feel

example, if you don't want that kitten of yours to climb onto the counter and help himself to some of your tuna fish sandwich, the best thing to do is to keep it away from him, where he can't reach it, and firmly tell him "No." Then, take him off the counter.

"This tastes terrible!" Cats will sometimes investigate objects by chewing on them.

Some people suggest that you should start your kitten off in a cage in your home, a place where he can be securely placed when he cannot be kept under your supervision. We disagree with this approach, but we do agree that no kitten should be given the run of the house on day one, or day two...or until he is ready for this kind of freedom. Newly born or very young kittens most certainly have to be closely watched and protected from themselves. They can get into all kinds of trouble if they are left alone unsupervised. Their sense of

balance hasn't been established yet, and because of this they're always climbing up banisters, sofas, stairways—and falling right back down. They are so small that they cannot be seen by the casual visitor to your home. They may be stepped on accidentally if they get caught underfoot. And the kitten may crawl under furniture and get into some restricted area he cannot squirm out of as easily as he managed to squirm into it. Kittens can get hurt or become frightened when they find themselves in such a tight squeeze.

But instead of a cage, we would recommend a room, with a door that can be closed, along with a litter pan and some drinking water and food. Then place the kitten in a box with sides just high enough so

"Newly born or very young kittens most certainly have to be protected from themselves."

As a new cat owner, you should be aware of your responsibility for your cat's safety and well-being.

that he feels secure. Kittens should be handled this way from the time they are very, very young until they are about six weeks of age.

LITTER PAN TRAINING

Not to be facetious, but the one who really needs "litter pan training" is the person who's taking care of the kitten. By this we mean that a kitten has a natural desire for cleanliness; he has already learned that from his mother. And in that respect, the kitten has come to expect very clean and sanitary surroundings for his toilet. Problems usually occur when the kitten's guardian fails to keep the litter pan and the litter inside it clean...or when the kitten's guardian fails to sweep up the area around the litter pan.

One of the big advantages of having a kitten in your

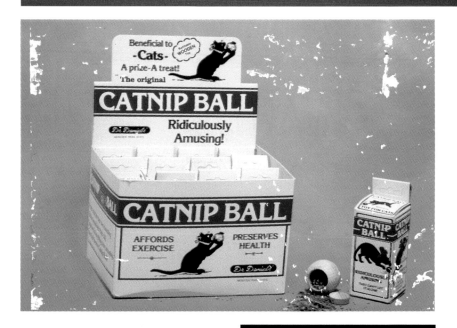

home is the fact that you don't have to walk it like you would a dog or a puppy. Many cats spend their entire lives indoors, and they are especially the right pet for people who live in apartment buildings. But because the kitten uses "indoor" facilities, it is up to you to make an extra effort to provide a sanitary, easily accessible "toilet," or litter pan.

Various types of litter pans are available at pet shops: rust-proof galvanized pans, heavy plastic litter pans, and enamel pans. You should decide what size litter pan is best for your kitten. If you have more than one feline in the house, you may want to do one of two things: use two separate litter pans, one for each kitten; or use a larger-than-average litter pan. Make sure the side panels are low enough for the kitten or kittens to climb over. As the kittens get older, you may

Catnip has long been a favorite with cats. You can purchase it encased in a ball, which will amuse your cat for hours on end. Photo courtesy Dr. A.C. Daniels.

Maine Coon. Making the trip to its new home can be unsettling for a little kitten, so when you first bring your pet home, keep things calm and quiet for him.

want to use a larger litter pan.

Whatever the size or type of pan (we should mention here that cardboard is not good, even as an emergency pan, as it absorbs moisture), you must be able to clean and deodorize it efficiently. It would be a good idea to wash out the litter pan with soap and hot water once a day. Never use chemical cleansers, ammonia, pine oil, etc. Your kitten uses his paws in the pan and will later clean them with his tongue. Cleaning the litter pan with soap and water will do just fine.

The idea is to establish a routine for both your kitten and yourself. If you clean the litter pan thoroughly at the end of each day as a regular chore, and then fill it with clean litter, your kitten will catch on to the program, and, in all likelihood, adjust his personal toilet habits accordingly. One thing's for sure: if you let that litter pan get dirty, your kitten will let you know about it either by using the floor right next to it, or by finding another, more sanitary spot in the house. And you really can't blame him for doing so.

Routine cleanliness. That's rule number one. Rule number two: keep that litter pan in one place. Don't keep moving it around, especially if you have a new kitten; you'll confuse your pet, and accidents will happen. We would suggest that you keep the litter pan

Japanese Bobtail, tricolor.

in an out-of-the-way but well-ventilated spot. For very young kittens, the litter pan should be very close to their sleeping quarters. If you want to move it as the kitten gets older, it might be a good idea to place it underneath a window, which you can keep open in the warmer weather, and shut in winter when those nasty drafts start to chill your home.

There will be mistakes at first, especially when the kitten is finding his way around his new home. He may accidentally soil carpets as he runs around. Make sure you clean and deodorize these spots; otherwise, they will be re-used for the same purpose.

What kind of litter should

"For very young kittens, the litter pan should be very close to their sleeping quarters."

This cat can enjoy sunshine and fresh air within the safe confines of his outdoor enclosure. The tree limb makes a handy scratching post.

you use? There are several different kinds, and they vary in price, ranging from economical to very expensive, from non-deodorizing to deodorizing. You have to be practical. If you have three or four kittens, or a kitten and a cat or two, in all likelihood, you really can't always buy the most expensive cat litter. It would cost you a fortune. Finding the right, but most economical for your budget, litter is a process of trial and error. Try a few different brands. See how your kittens like each brand; see if you can detect any difference in the way each absorbs litter pan odors. Avoid using very dusty litter. It will make your kitten, and you, cough.

> **"...kittens are very clean animals that like their surroundings, their litter pans, and themselves to be spotless."**

Give your kitten a decent amount of litter so that he can bury his wastes and still walk away from a clean litter pan.

We would also recommend that you keep the immediate area surrounding the litter pan clean by frequent sweeping and mopping. Some people recommend that a plastic litter liner be placed on the bottom of the litter pan before it is filled with litter. You might also consider applying the same principle to the larger area underneath and surrounding the litter pan: place the litter pan on a layer of plastic, and by doing so, you will keep your floors from getting soiled in spots.

And still another precaution you can take to keep the area surrounding the litter pan clean is to use the totally enclosed litter pan; it provides your cat with a real sense of privacy

This cat is allowed outdoors on a regular basis. Its owner has attached an ID tag to its collar should it stray too far from home and be found by someone else.

Some houseplants can be poisonous, so use caution in this regard when it comes to your cat.

and keeps all of the litter in the pan.

OTHER LITTER-RELATED PROBLEMS

Yes, kittens are very clean animals that like their surroundings, their litter pans, and themselves to be spotless. However, you may run into what might appear to be a contradiction of this behavior. Your kitten may begin to use different spots in your home for his toilet, even though you have kept his litter pan spotless. There are several possible explanations for this kind of behavior. If something's upsetting your kitten, he might do this. An older cat might do this if a new kitten is introduced to the home— and to him—too quickly. Cats will, if they perceive danger of any kind, begin an all-out "war" to mark their territories. In other instances, unaltered cats who start hanging around your front door or porch may upset your cats. So, we might add a third rule for a clean feline environment: make sure that relations between your cats are good, and set up some good barriers between the neighborhood cats outside and your own cats. Try not to create a situation in which your cat is forced to establish and mark his territory.

CLAWED OR DECLAWED?

There is considerable disagreement on the subject of having a cat's claws removed—having him or her "de-clawed." It is often a

Cats are remarkably agile and will leap from one spot to another with the greatest of ease. If there are certain areas of your home that you want to be off-limits for your cat, establish "house rules" while you cat is still a kitten.

Special doors such as this enable pets to come and go at will. Fortunately, this cat has access only to an enclosed courtyard, in which it can safely enjoy the outdoors.

"Cats will, if they perceive danger of any kind, begin an all-out 'war' to mark their territories."

hotly debated subject. First of all, the reason a cat has claws is to defend himself; also to climb trees; and to catch prey. Therefore, in his natural environment, the

kitten or cat without claws would be at a serious disadvantage; you might say he would be very handicapped. If you plan to let your kitten or cat outdoors, you should not have him or her de-clawed.

But if you plan to keep your pet indoors all the time, then it may be something to consider...but still only as a last resort.

The reason people would consider it in the first place is because the kitten or cat will tend to scratch and claw at rugs, carpets, the backs of chairs and sofas, mattresses, and similar items. It is not a purposefully destructive act on the part of the animal; it is an instinctive act.

THE SCRATCHING POST

One way to come to grips with your feline's urge to claw is to provide the animal with a scratching post. Scratching posts can be

A scratching post is an important item in every cat owner's inventory. It will help to reduce the chances of the cat's damaging furniture and draperies. Photo courtesy of Four Paws.

Areas such as this should be off limits to your cat.

If you are not sure about how to clip your kitten's claws, perhaps your vet can show you how. Acclimating a kitten to claw clipping will make the procedure a lot more tolerable as the animal matures.

purchased at any pet shop. Some kittens will know what it's for and take to it like a fighter to a punching bag; others have to be shown what it's for. When the kitten starts scratching your sofa or other household furnishings, hold him up to the scratching post and carefully place his paws against it. Once he gets the idea, he may forget all about *your* furniture and carpeting and stick to his own special furniture. If he continues to ignore the scratching post, cover it with a piece of carpet that has been rubbed with catnip.

Keeping your kitten's claws trimmed is another way to reduce the wear and tear he will cause on your furniture and carpets. Claws can be clipped every few weeks. It is advisable to start doing this when the kitten is showing his first interest in your furniture. Don't just take out an old pair of scissors from the kitchen or

bathroom and go to work. Stop by your local pet shop and pick up a pair of small clippers suitable for kittens and cats.

Before you begin, make sure that your kitten is relaxed. Take off just a bit of claw at a time and make sure that you don't accidentally cut into the "quick," the pink area under the claw. This is fed by a vein and if cut will create much bleeding. Look closely and you will see that pink vein. Stay away from it with those clippers. Turn the kitten's paw sideways. Apply pressure on the paw to extend the claws. Then clip off just the tip of the claws. Your pet's claws need not be trimmed on a regular basis: trim them only as necessary.

This bi-level scratching post can accommodate several cats. For variety, it is covered with carpeting and sisal.

Burmese. How exciting it is to see your purebred kitten develop the markings and characteristics of its breed.

KITTENS TODAY

FEEDING

Only you can ensure that your pet grows up to be the strong, healthy cat that he is capable of becoming physically and mentally. His first year is an important one; and, with proper diet and care, you can help start your kitten off on the road to good health. The correct diet will help your kitten to develop strong bones, good teeth, and a lustrous coat.

Kittens are much like babies: they need to eat and drink a lot—three, four, or five times a day. Little portions are the rule here. You don't want to let your kitten's stomach start "growling" from a lack of food, but you don't want to serve king-size portions either.

Each kitten should have his own dish (dishes, really): one for food and one for water. Wash your kitten's dishes with hot soapy water after each feeding, as you would your dishes. It's easy to forget to do this, to get lazy, and simply add food to the food left behind from the previous meal, but that can lead to upset stomachs and finicky eaters. Do not try to

"Let's eat!" This hungry gang of cats will polish off their meal in no time flat.

save leftovers until the next meal, even if some food must be wasted. Of course, dry food can be left in the dish a little longer, but it,

"Wash your kitten's dishes with hot soapy water after each feeding, as you would your dishes."

too, should be discarded each day. A routine, such as the one you establish for litter box maintenance, can be set up. At the end of each day, before you go to sleep, make sure that the dishes are clean. Don't forget to replenish the drinking water. When you get up in the morning, serve the first meal of the day in a perfectly spotless dish or bowl. The dish will be clean, and the food will be perfectly fresh to start the kitten off on his busy day. Soon he will learn to appreciate this kind of service.

Fundamentally, cats are carnivores, or meat eaters.

In their wild state, they usually devour the entire carcass of their prey, including skin, internal organs, bones, and whatever greens the prey may have eaten. In this way, cats in the wild achieve a nutritionally balanced diet. Since your kitten will be indoors, it will not be encountering

"Fundamentally, cats are carnivores, or meat eaters."

This striking Maine Coon radiates every appearance of good health. If you familiarize yourself with the basics of feline nutrition, you should be able to provide a good diet for your kitten.

Just as with other kinds of pets, obesity in cats is to be discouraged. The right diet and regular exercise can help to prevent this problem.

any wild game. Therefore, it's important to learn about proper nutrition. Your kitten is depending on you to provide for it now that it is in *your* environment. It should be noted that here we are talking about feeding kittens eight weeks of age and older.

VARIETIES OF CATFOOD

There are four basic kinds of commercial cat food to choose from: canned, specialty, dry, and semi-moist.

Canned cat food usually contains about 10 percent protein, 2 percent fat, and 75 percent moisture. Most canned cat foods supply complete nutrition, although the meat content may be lower than in specialty cat food.

Specialty cat food, usually offered in little flat cans, usually contains from 10 to 25 percent protein, 2 to 5 percent fat, and about 75 percent moisture. Some of these specialty dishes will really whet your kitten's appetite. They are all-meat dishes, containing about 95 percent meat product. While this type of food contains all of the protein a kitten needs, it doesn't provide other nutrients. Specialty cat foods, which come in several different flavors, should be used as a food supplement.

Dry cat food usually contains these other nutrients needed by your kitten. Dry cat food also contains meat. Many people prefer it for its convenience: It is less "messy" than canned food.

Semi-moist cat food, available in individual sealed pouches, usually contains 25 percent protein, 7 percent fat, and 33 percent moisture.

The most important thing regarding your pet's diet is *balance.* I would not recommend an over-reliance on any one of these food types but instead would offer various combinations of them.

Let your kitten try all kinds of food. You'll soon know what he likes and dislikes by what's left on his plate.

> **Several cats and their puppy pal enjoy a leisurely meal together. It is important that you establish a regular feeding schedule for your pet.**

MILK

There are several schools of thought on this subject. Some people say that it was made for cats—and that cats will love it all of their lives. Others have observed that milk and other diary products upset the kitten's stomach, causing diarrhea. Therefore, be forewarned that if you offer milk to your pet, the animal may be subject to bouts of this illness. If given, milk should always be served fresh. Remember that milk is a food and should *never* be substituted for water.

WATER

Water is nature's means of cleansing the body of

"Let your kitten try all kinds of food. You'll soon know what he likes and dislikes by what's left on his plate."

"...Remember that all cats have individual tastes."

Himalayan kittens eagerly awaiting their dinner. Kittens need to be fed several times a day.

wastes. Your kitten should have access to clean fresh water at all times. The water bowl should be thoroughly cleaned on a regular basis to prevent any build-up of bacteria.

TABLE SCRAPS

Moderation is the key when it comes to feeding table scraps. A bit of broiled flounder or a few bites of roasted chicken or turkey will almost certainly be relished by a cat, and such foods are nutritious as well. Overly salty or sugary items will do little, if anything, to fortify the feline diet. In general, consider table scraps as treats, not the mainstay of your cat's diet. And *never* feed your cat any food that has bones in it: they can splinter and cause injury and even death.

Finally, remember that all cats have individual tastes. Their food preferences may depend on aroma, taste, or consistency.

Ideally, what you want to see is a healthy appetite: you want to see your kitten run to its food dish and polish off its meal with gusto. Proper weight, bright clear eyes, a nice coat, and unblemished skin are some of the best indications that your kitten is getting all the nutrition he needs.

A cat must have access to fresh clean water at all times.

KITTENS TODAY

CHOOSING THE RIGHT VETERINARIAN

T he veterinarian is going to be your kitten's best friend, next to you, of course! Today, veterinarians are highly skilled and trained to deliver good health care to your pet. However, there are a number of factors to consider when choosing the *right* veterinarian for you— and your pet.

An important consideration is to select a vet who has been *recommended* to you by satisfied cat owners. (Some veterinarians may specialize in different types of pets.) And, as in the case of selecting a physician for yourself, you should take into account your vet's "bedside manner." Is he cold to you, and to your kitten? Does he *like* kittens? You treat your kitten very nicely, and you want to be sure that your vet will do so too. You want to bring your kitten to a vet who is as fond of animals, especially kittens, as you are. And you want to see that the receptionists, technicians, and others who work in that

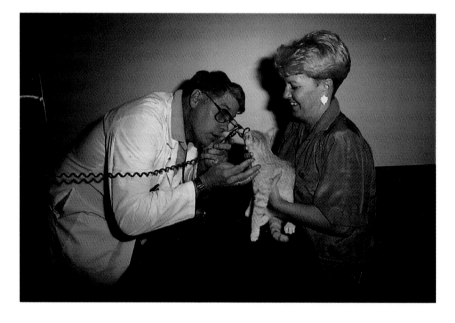

vet's office also take a special interest in all of the animals that they treat.

The vet's office should, of course, be spotless. Basically, you want your vet—and all of the people who work for him—to "go the extra mile" for you and your pet. You want to know that when your kitten is in need of treatment, they will all go out of their way to do all that they can to help.

Recommendations from other people are very important because you may find that the vet you just picked out of the phone

Taking your cat for regular veterinary check-ups is one of the most important things that you can do to safeguard your cat's health.

"Today, veterinarians are highly skilled and trained to deliver good health care to your pet."

book charges unreasonably high fees for his services. You want, of course, only the best for your kitten, but that does not mean that you should just sit back and accept unusually high prices and surcharges for your vet's services. Just because a particular vet charges a lot more for his services doesn't mean that you are "getting the best." As is the case with most everything, prices do vary. A little bit of advice, though: don't wait for an emergency before you start shopping around. You should find out as soon as possible who in

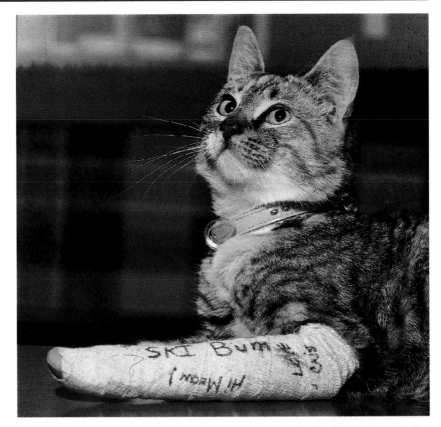

"Once upon a time, the family physician used to make house calls. Believe it or not, there are still some veterinarians who provide this kind of medical service."

your area is the best vet.

Once upon a time, the family physician used to make house calls. Believe it or not, there are still some veterinarians who provide this kind of medical service. And, you will be pleased to hear, if you are fortunate enough to have a vet like this in your area, that his services may not be as expensive as you might think for providing that extra service. In fact, you may even save yourself some time and money and unnecessary worrying and waiting if you can avail yourself of a house call for your pet. Vets who make house calls can keep down the cost of running their operations by cutting down on overhead; they don't have the expense of the office and

Despite a cat's agility and prowess, accidents can happen. This cat is recovering from a broken leg sustained in a fall.

the large staff. They can pass on these savings to you. Of course, you must understand that we are speaking here of the veterinarian who provides fairly routine services: shots, check-ups, prescriptions, and preliminary diagnoses. For major medical procedures, you will, of course, need to bring your kitten to the office or, if necessary, animal hospital. But the vet who can provide routine procedures in your home is going to be very, very helpful to you and your pet.

Consider the logic to this approach: think about how nervous you are when you have to go to a doctor's office or a hospital—for anything, however minor. And then think about how terrified your tiny kitten will be when he has to go to the veterinarian's office, where he may encounter, probably for the first time, that huge German Shepherd Dog in the waiting room...And what about all of those strange animal scents! Your kitten may be a sociable fellow when company comes, but he can certainly do without this kind of visit. At home, your kitten is naturally much more relaxed—in fact, he should be totally relaxed—and he should also be used to visitors from time to time. (If not, you should help him with that.) The vet can walk right into your home and meet your kitten in "his" home: in the

kitchen, the garage, out on the front porch, or wherever your kitten normally "hangs out." The vet can take a look at him; perhaps slip some medicine into his favorite food; and very, very casually give him a shot or two with very little fuss and fanfare.

Having a vet that makes house calls is a tremendous advantage for the multi-cat or multi-pet household. Have you ever tried transporting more than one cat to a vet? You'd probably have to make more than one trip. Recently, all of our cats had to be inoculated. The vet came to the house; and in ten minutes the cats had their shots, and

A veterinary technician tidies up the office between patients. When selecting a vet, you should try to choose one that has been recommended to you by satisfied cat owners.

everyone then went on his merry way.

If you can find a vet who will make house calls for a reasonable price, consider yourself very fortunate and by all means (again, if he is highly recommended by other animal lovers like you) take advantage of this wonderful pet health care service.

The vet that you choose should be someone you can depend on to prescribe and diagnose with skill and to handle both your kitten— and you—with sympathetic understanding. Your vet should be someone who will know how you, as a lover of animals, can be burdened with worry and anxiety when you pet is ill or seems out of sorts. From the moment that you step into his office, or he walks through your front door, your vet will be the one person who will help take that heavy burden off your shoulders, and whatever happens will give you the feeling that you are giving your kitten the very best health care possible.

A final health care tip that can prove very valuable: write up a proper vaccination schedule, list shots required to keep your kitten safe from the various feline diseases, and note health problems commonly associated with cats. This is especially important for multi-pet households where communicable disease can be brought into the house by other pets.

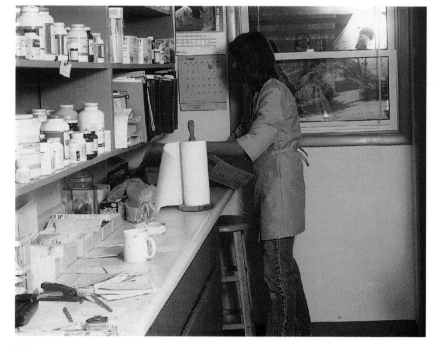

KITTENS TODAY

SPAYING AND NEUTERING

Before we discuss the details of when and where to spay or neuter your cat, something should be said about the tragic overpopulation of cats. Cats are extremely prolific. According to SPCA statistics, a female cat that is not spayed will produce 12 offspring a year. If each of these 12 produces young in like quantity, the result would be 144 offspring. Simple multiplication illustrates the rapid growth rate of the cat population. Sadly, it is impossible to find homes for all of these cats.

It is unnecessary for you to feel that your cat should not be spayed so that she may have the "experience" of motherhood (she does not need to), and there are more than enough kittens in the world so that everyone who wants one can have one.

Unless you have a pedigreed cat and are planning to breed it, you must without fail neuter the male or spay the female. These safe surgical procedures will go a long way toward simplifying your feline's care throughout its entire life by removing, once and for all, that instinctive

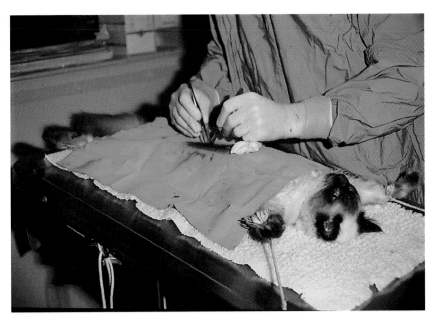

urge to run out of the house periodically to fight and cavort with other cats. As a sidelight to this, cats, when they are mating, chase one another around the neighborhood and are not as cautious crossing the street as they normally would be.

You will be doing your cat a big favor: you will be helping to keep it out of all kinds of trouble and danger by having it altered. If you feel that in doing so you are, in a sense, depriving the cat of part of life's natural experience, don't. Altered, the cat will not even know the difference; he or she will be very content and happy in your home.

This cat is undergoing a spay operation. This procedure requires an overnight stay at the vet's.

"Unless you have a pedigreed cat and are planning to breed it, you must without fail neuter the male or spay the female."

NEUTERING THE MALE

Neutering, or castration, of the male is usually performed before he reaches his eighth or ninth month of age. Let your veterinarian or animal clinic decide the exact time that this should be done. You can save money by having your pet altered at a well-run animal clinic that performs such services, usually with the overall good of the pet community in mind. It is a fairly simple operation, and it will usually require an overnight stay for your pet. Do not put it off. It must be done before the male kitten gets any ideas about roaming the neighborhood in search of a female. A mature, unaltered tomcat has an almost uncontrollable urge to roam and fight. And his litter box will always have a strong odor. If you have an unaltered male cat and you keep him indoors most of the time, he may develop the annoying habit of spraying your walls and furniture with urine as he gets older— from a year to two years of age. The spray can ruin home furnishings, and the odor is very unpleasant and difficult, if not impossible, to get rid of. Some psychologists say this spraying by the male cat is his method of marking his territory (something he will feel much less compelled to do after he's been desexed). In fact, after he's been altered, your male cat will make an even better pet

These two farm cats mated shortly after this photo was taken. Unfortunately, there are not enough homes to go around for all the kittens that are born each year.

than he is now; he will express his vitality and energy in play rather than hostility. He will not undergo the anxiety and stress, the aggressiveness and howling, and the other ramifications of his mating activities.

"Spaying will not alter the female's disposition, except to make her less nervous, less noisy, more relaxed, and more playful and affectionate."

SPAYING THE FEMALE

Many veterinarians feel that the ideal age for spaying is about six to eight months of age because the female has had her first heat (her first seasonal period) by that time. You don't want to have your feline spayed too early. There's danger that the young female kitten will not have a chance to fully develop.

Spaying involves an anesthetic, an abdominal incision, and an overnight stay at the vet's or at the animal spay clinic. After going home and until the stitches are removed, activity should be restricted and care taken to see that the kitten does not break open the incision.

Spaying will not alter the female's disposition, except to make her less nervous, less noisy, more relaxed, and more playful and affectionate. She may possibly put on some weight and get a little rounder in the pouch, but proper diet and exercise will keep her energetic, sleek, and muscular—the way she's supposed to be. Spaying your female kitten will also keep the local toms from coming around, howling outside your window and spraying and possibly killing your shrubs.

Also, unless you have your female spayed, she may be in recurring heat, not just a few times a year but as often as every three or four weeks, and she will exhaust herself each time she follows her natural desire to mate.

How do you know your female is in heat? She'll start rolling around on the ground and will become more affectionate than usual. If you have male cats, even desexed ones, she'll make her intentions known to them in unmistakable ways. If they have been desexed, they will consider her a nuisance and not their normal playmate. They'll want to play as usual and fight or wrestle: she'll want to mate. And they will try to avoid her when she's like this. Her voice will also change, becoming more of a demanding

A Siamese and an Oriental Shorthair. Both are almost fully mature.

The female cat is anesthetized before an incision is made in her abdomen.

howl. And don't forget about the all-night howling from all the males in the neighborhood who can sense that a female— even indoors—is in heat. And prepare for some frightening sounds as the males in the neighborhood fight over this female.

The importance of spaying the female cannot be overemphasized. Kittens are produced in such great numbers that there simply are not enough homes for them to go around. By seeing to it that your kitten will be incapable of adding to an already over-populated world of helpless kittens, you will be doing a good deed for your pet and for the animal community itself.

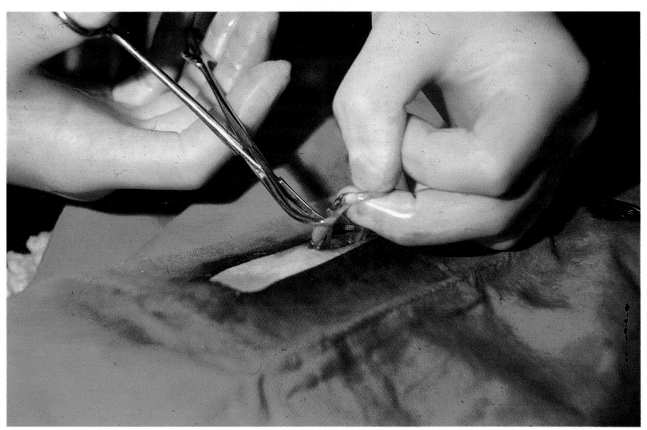

KITTENS TODAY

HEALTH CARE

C ats are basically strong, healthy animals that can take care of themselves. However, there are certain diseases, illnesses, and afflictions to which a cat is subject. This is where you will have to help out. The first thing for you to do is to bring your new kitten to your veterinarian for a complete check-up. He may suggest inoculations against panleukopenia (also known as infectious enteritis or feline distemper) and rabies. He may also be able to detect if your kitten needs to be de-wormed.

PANLEUKOPENIA

Panleukopenia is a very serious and contagious disease among cats and has a very high mortality rate. The best step you can take to prevent your kitten from becoming afflicted with this dreadful disease is to have him inoculated against it. Cats nine weeks of age and older should be inoculated and should be given a booster shot each year after that.

An infected kitten will run a very high fever, perhaps as high as 105 degrees. He will lose his appetite but at the

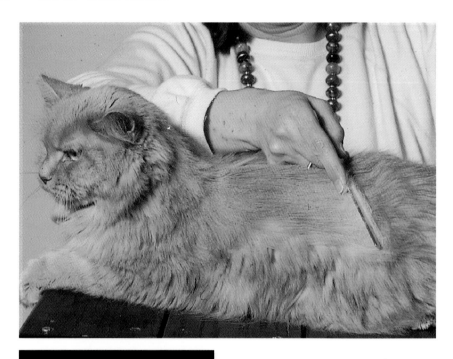

When you groom your cat, you should check for fleas and ticks, as well as for any skin disorders.

same time have an intense thirst for water in an attempt to compensate for the dehydration that he is experiencing. The infected kitten may also become prone to diarrhea or vomiting spells that will continue to weaken him and make him more listless. If your kitten has this disease, it must be quarantined from other cats.

Again, make sure that your kitten is given shots to prevent panleukopenia.

"The first thing for you to do is to bring your new kitten to your veterinarian for a complete check-up."

Keep accurate records of these inoculations as well as follow-up booster shots.

RABIES

If your cats stay indoors all of the time, they will be far less prone to contracting rabies than cats who go outdoors. Rabies can be contracted from other cats or from various wildlife species. Again, the best way to safeguard your cat is to have him inoculated against this illness. Some municipalities provide free yearly rabies shots for cats, as well as for dogs.

URINARY PROBLEMS

Cats can become afflicted with various urinary problems, some of which may stem from an overdependence on dry cat food. Stones form in the urinary tract much in the same way that kidney stones do in man. Male cats are more prone to urinary problems than are female cats.

If your cat has trouble urinating or seems to be spending more time in the litter box than it normally does, waste no time in taking it to the vet. Such symptoms could be the first stage of a urinary problem that may, if not treated in time, cause death.

WORMS

Some kittens have worms during the first few months of their lives. This is especially true in the case

of strays. Be sure to have the veterinarian check your kitten for worms. Many kinds of worms can be found in the feces, so you'll be asked to bring in a stool sample.

The following intestinal parasites can be treated with great success by your vet.

Hookworms

There are several species of hookworms that can infect cats. Infested animals appear anemic with possible respiratory problems. These worms can be destroyed with chemicals administered by your vet.

Roundworms

These parasites are the most common form of worm in kittens. Symptoms of roundworm may include dull coat, pot belly, listlessness, or failure to grow at a normal rate. There may also be digestive problems, and the kitten

Cat dental kits are available to help fight plaque, reduce tartar build-up, and control unpleasant breath. Photo courtesy of Four Paws.

may vomit. Roundworms may be seen in a microscopic examination of the infected cat's feces. There are several drugs that are very effective in the treatment of this parasite.

Tapeworms

There are many types of tapeworm that may infest your kitten. Segments of these parasites may be seen in the stool. Symptoms include a ruffled coat, a general sickly appearance, and irritability.

Tapeworms may sometimes be transmitted to your cat by an infected flea. Your cat may bite at the flea and accidentally ingest it. The tapeworm eggs may hatch inside your cat. Evidence of tapeworm infestation is often evidenced by rice-like particles on your pet or on the floors. There is a medication that the vet can give you to eliminate this problem; however, infestation may reoccur if the flea problem is not treated as well.

Fleas and Ticks

You can suspect flea infestation when your cat starts to scratch a lot. Fleas are blood-sucking parasites that can multiply on your cat—and in your home—at an incredible rate. If you allow them to go unchecked, they can

Pet shops carry a wide variety of fine products that will help to keep your cat's coat looking its best. Photo courtesy of Four Paws.

Vitamin/mineral and other food supplements are formulated for general nutritional enhancement or to serve particular purposes, such as skin and coat enhancement and/or flea and tick control. Photo courtesy of Four Paws.

transmit other parasites to your pet.

Fleas plague even the most scrupulously clean cats and the cleanest of homes, especially when the heat and humidity start to rise.

A number of different strategies can be used to prevent fleas from becoming a major problem. You can put a flea collar on your cat. Fleas like to settle under your cat's chin, near the ears, and throughout his undercoat.

Another way to kill fleas is to bring your cat to the groomer for a shampoo; or, if you are experienced enough, you can shampoo kitty yourself. Pet shops carry a wide variety of flea sprays and powders that also can be effective in your flea-prevention program. Some homes are so badly infested with fleas that the residents call an exterminator and order a flea "bombing." This should be a last resort. Once you have solved the flea problem, you must still go to work destroying any eggs that may be embedded in your carpeting, in crevices, and in those out-of-the-way places where your kitten likes to play. Another very good means of keeping fleas in check is to keep an eye out for them when you are grooming your cat.

Ticks are not as common as fleas, but when they do appear, they can present bigger problems. When they attach themselves to your cat's skin, they can cause infection, fever, anemia, and even more serious conditions. The tick bites deeply into its host and begins to swell with the animal's blood. If you attempt to pull the tick out, you must be sure to remove it entirely. If the head remains embedded in the cat's skin, infection may result. After you have removed the tick, clean the affected area with alcohol-dampened cotton. You can also purchase preventive sprays and powders to ward off ticks.

HAIRBALLS

All cats are plagued to some extent by hairballs. You can help to solve this problem by regularly grooming your cat. This is

Cats that are allowed to roam at will are exposed to a number of dangers.

Gentle and effective in elimination of swallowed hair & the prevention of hair balls

Elimination Of Hair Balls In Cats And Kittens

NET WT. 1.75 OZS. (49.6g)

Products are available for the prevention and treatment of hair balls. They can help to prevent constipation and to eliminate any accumulated hair. Photo courtesy of Four Paws.

especially necessary if your feline is a longhair. Your cat sheds most of the time, but you will especially notice it in spring, summer, and fall; you'll start to find hairs on you kitten's bed, on his favorite chair, and throughout the house. Shedding is a natural process: the thick winter coat is shed in summer so that the animal can be comfortable.

Your cat may rub itself along your floor or your carpet in an attempt to rid itself of any scratchy hair, and it will continue to lick its coat at the same time. It starts to ingest the hair that is being shed. If the cat swallows enough hair, the hair will form knots in the animal's stomach and intestines to such a degree that they can interfere with normal body functions. Coughing, vomiting, gagging, or constipation may occur if the hairball starts to build up. Along with frequent brushing, a hairball remedy is a good way of keeping this problem in check.

You may also want to do an extra special job of cleaning your floors and vacuuming your carpeting when your cat is shedding.

KITTENS TODAY

KITTENS ON THE WAY?

I have addressed the need to have your kitten spayed or neutered, and perhaps you have been planning to have this done. Your female, however, has managed to slip out of the house; and with time, her increasing girth indicates that she is expecting...If this is, indeed, the case, you have some work to do. First of all, you should contact your vet and plan accordingly for any problems that might arise relating to the care of the mother and her babies.

Mother cats *usually* take care of their kittens, but there are times when the youngsters are abandoned. Or, what about this scenario? Let's say a stray cat has given birth to a litter in your backyard and you want to help out...

In either case, you will want to be prepared to care for the newborns should the need arise. So, let's review what happens during a cat's pregnancy and what to expect after the kittens arrive.

HEAT, OR ESTRUS

The female cat's heat, or estrus, period begins when her vulva begins to swell; her appetite starts to increase, and she may develop a restless disposition. Male cats in the neighborhood will sense this, and you'll start to hear howling outside your windows day and night, as they attempt to "serenade" her. When *she* is ready for mating, *she'll* start howling—or calling for a mate. She'll become much more affectionate than usual and you may see her rolling about on the ground. It is at this time that she will mate with the male—or males— of *her* choice. (The kittens in any one litter can have more than one father.) The gestation period is about 63 days, although it may be a few days shorter or a few days longer.

Be sure that the queen is fed a well-balanced diet. Check with the vet about offering her a vitamin/mineral supplement. Until the last week of her pregnancy, she can live her life pretty much the way she has been doing prior to her pregnancy.

In the last week of her pregnancy, the female will start to slow down a little. She may seem very busy

trying to find a nice safe place to give birth. At this time, you should introduce her to the kittening box.

A kittening, or maternity, box should be used while the kittens are being born and during the time they are nursing. The box should be large enough so that the mother can stretch out at full length on her side and have room to spare near her head and tail. The floor of the box should be lined with shredded paper and a clean towel. Make sure that you put the box in a quiet, warm, draft-free location—away from the family's usual traffic patterns. Now allow nature to take its course.

DELIVERY

Prior to the birth of the kittens, you should verify with your vet that some kind assistance will be available if it is needed.

The average kitten litter consists of four to six kittens. The normal birth is head first, with paws alongside the head. Each kitten will arrive completely enclosed in a semi-transparent membrane. You will see

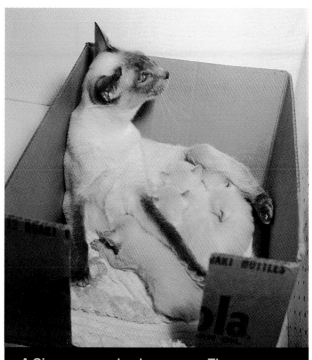

A Siamese nursing her young. These youngsters will be fully weaned by eight weeks of age.

Most female cats are instinctively good mothers and will provide the proper care for their kittens.

If a kitten is orphaned before the age of eight weeks, it will have to be hand-fed and will need attention much like that given to a newborn baby.

These hungry kittens are totally oblivious to their mother's efforts to groom them. Kittens will be able to drink from a saucer when they are about two to three weeks of age.

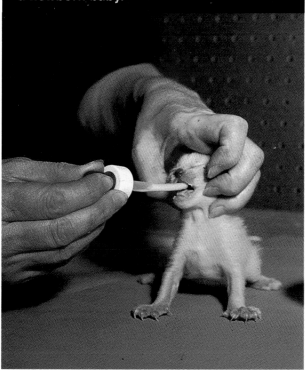

the kitten and the umbilical cord. The mother will tear the sac from around the kitten and nip the umbilical cord. She will clean the kitten all over. Don't worry if she seems to be a little rough: she is stimulating the kitten's circulatory and respiratory systems, much the same way a doctor does when he gives a newborn baby a whack.

Kittens are born completely helpless. They can't hear, see, or stand on their feet. All they know is the warmth of their mother's teats as they nuzzle up to her to nurse at short intervals day and night.

The senses of smell and taste are acquired in a few days. Then the protective seal on the ears breaks, and the babies can hear. The eyes, in most cases tightly shut at birth, open at about the ninth day, but time must pass before they can focus and really see. Kittens' newly opened eyes are sensitive to light and glare, so be sure to keep the kittening box out of bright light or direct sunlight.

At four weeks of age, the kittens are quite well developed and from that time on their growth is rapid. Mother cats instinctively know the care that their young ones need. They are ready and willing to nurse their kittens for a full eight weeks—the "basic training" of kittens, you might say. After eight weeks, kittens are ready to go to their new homes.

In the meantime, they develop by staying close to their mother for food and warmth. By about the fourth or fifth week, they start to get their baby teeth. At this time, the kittens will begin nibbling on solid food. By the time they are weaned, they will have become completely accustomed to solid food and will be able to eat dry chow formulated for kittens.

It is important that the kittens receive a sufficient supply of milk from their mother. You will be able to tell if they do not, because they will mew almost constantly and will be generally uneasy. If this is happening, call your vet. He will be able to advise you as to whether the kitten's diet should be supplemented.

ORPHANED KITTENS

By the age of eight weeks, the kitten should be weaned. But if a kitten has been orphaned or taken from the mother earlier than this age, you will have to do the feeding. Your vet will be able to recommend the best feeding program and will probably prescribe a kitten milk formula. If the kitten is still too small to drink from a saucer, you will have to give it milk from a medicine dropper...or by having it lick drops of milk from the tip of your finger. There are also miniature bottles with nipples that can be used to feed a newborn kitten.

During the first week, the kittens normally should be fed every two or three hours around the clock. After one week of age, the night feedings can usually be discontinued. When the kittens are two and a half to three weeks old, you can dab a little milk around their mouths. By licking the milk off of their faces, the kittens will learn how to lap milk from a saucer.

When they start showing interest in solid food, you can offer them small portions of high-quality kitten food. If the food is of the dry variety, you can moisten it with water. For variety, you can also offer baby cereal to the kittens.

At around eight weeks of age, you can reduce the number of feedings to four servings per day, depending on the individual appetite. Some kittens may want to eat a little more; others may want to eat a little less. When they reach the age of four to five months, they will be eating three meals daily. Cats that are fully mature should be fed twice a day.

INDEX

KITTENS TODAY